The Urbana Free Library

To renew: call **217-367-4057**
or go to **urbanafreelibrary.org**
and select **My Account**

LEFT and Right

A CRABTREE SEEDLINGS BOOK

Taylor Farley

CRABTREE
PUBLISHING COMPANY
WWW.CRABTREEBOOKS.COM

I know my left and right!

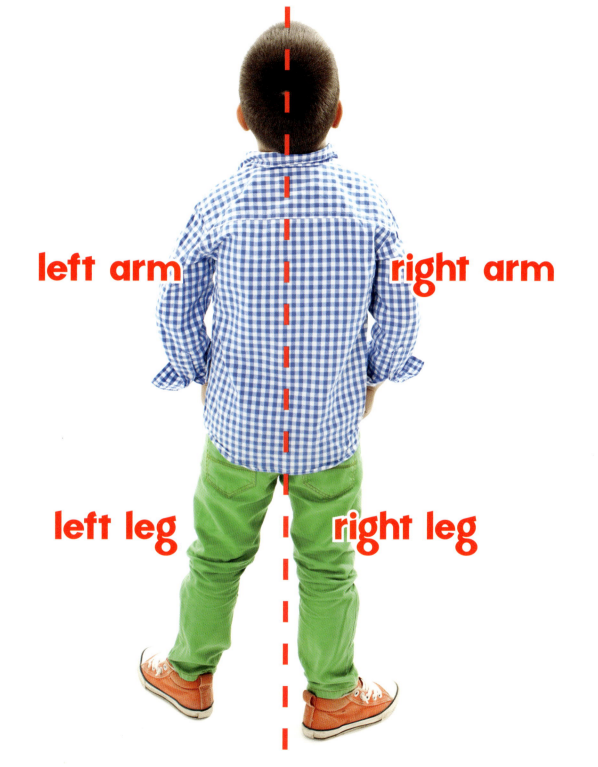

left arm

right arm

left leg

right leg

3

4

My left hand looks like the letter L.

I color with
my left hand.

My friend colors
with her right hand.

left hand

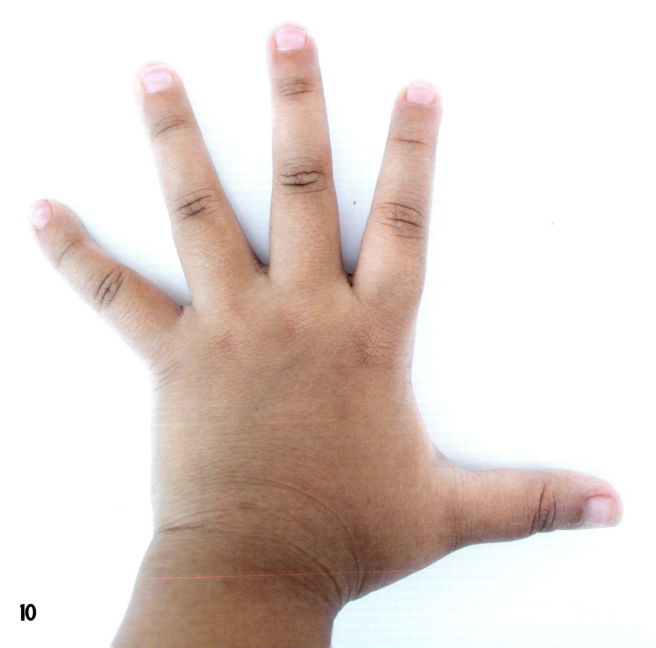

right hand

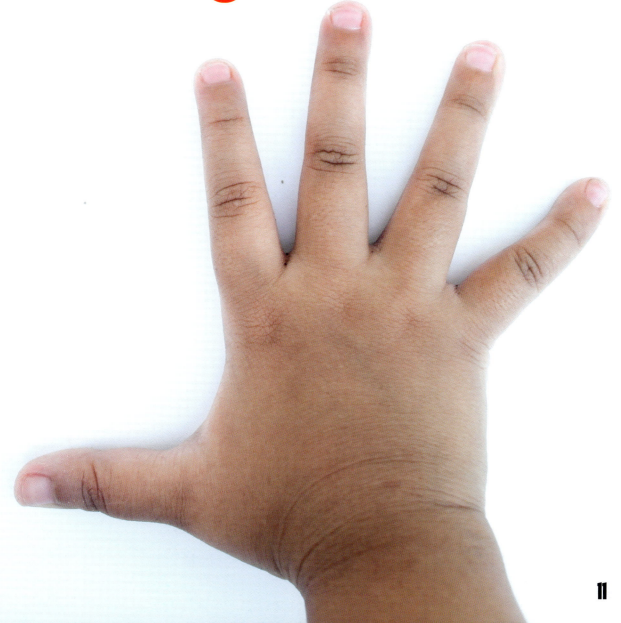

I ride my scooter.
I push with my
left foot.

left foot

13

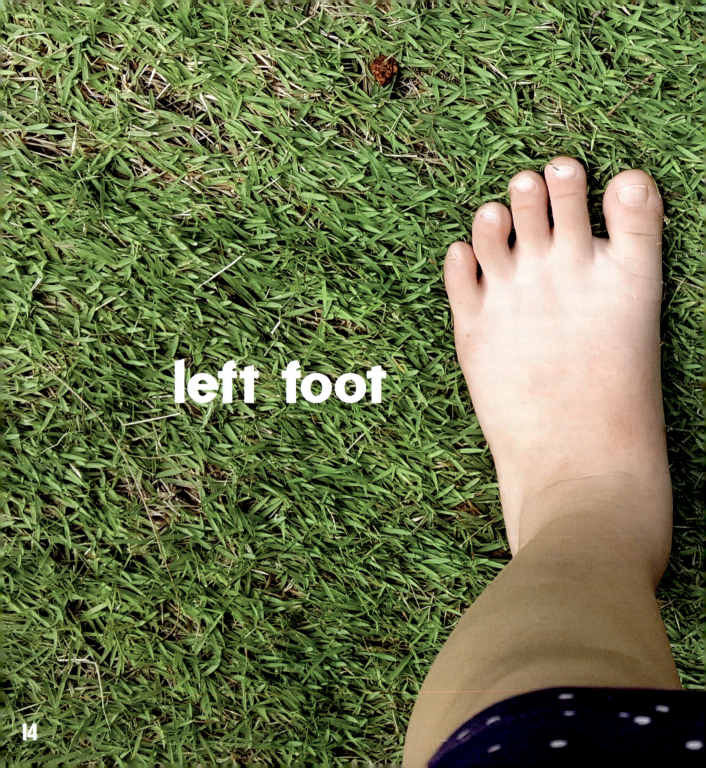

left foot

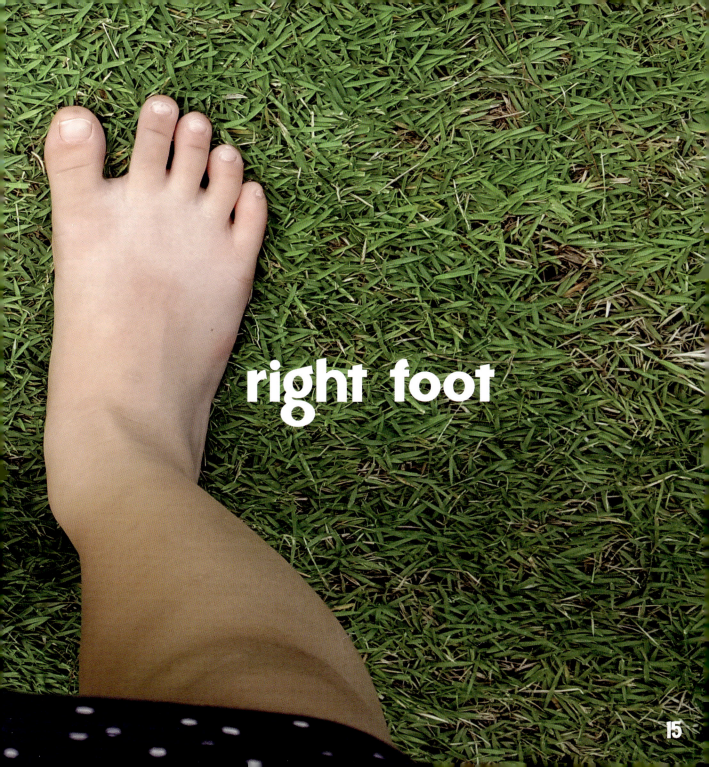

right foot

left shoe

right shoe

We want to cross
the road.

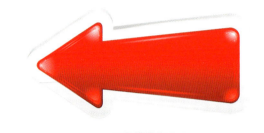

We look left.

We look right.

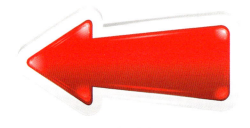

We look left again.

23

School-to-Home Support for Caregivers and Teachers

Crabtree Seedlings books help children grow by letting them practice reading. Here are a few guiding questions to help the reader with building his or her comprehension skills. Possible answers are included.

Before Reading

- What do I think this book is about? I think this book is about the directions left and right.

- What do I want to learn about this topic? I want to learn why it is important to know which direction is left and which direction is right.

During Reading

- I wonder why... I wonder why some people color with their left hand and others color with their right hand.

- What have I learned so far? I have learned that it is important to look left and right before crossing the road.

After Reading

- What details did I learn about this topic? I learned that we can tell which direction is left and which direction is right by looking at our hands, feet, and shoes.

- Write down unfamiliar words and ask questions to help understand their meaning. I see the word **scooter** on page 12. I see a picture of a girl riding her scooter. It looks like a skateboard with a handle and three wheels instead of four. Why is it called a scooter?

Library and Archives Canada Cataloging-in-Publication Data

Title: Left and right / Taylor Farley.
Names: Farley, Taylor, author.
Description: Series statement: Early learning concepts | "A Crabtree seedlings book". | Previously
  published in electronic format by Blue Door Education in 2020.
Identifiers: Canadiana 20200385542 | ISBN 9781427128447 (hardcover) | ISBN 9781427128522 (softcover)
Subjects: LCSH: Left and right (Psychology)—Juvenile literature.
Classification: LCC BF637.L36 F37 2021 | DDC j152.3/35—dc23

Library of Congress Cataloging-in-Publication Data

Names: Farley, Taylor, author.
Title: Left and right / Taylor Farley.
Description: New York : Crabtree Publishing, 2021. | Series: Early learning concepts : a Crabtree seedlings book
Identifiers: LCCN 2020049618 | ISBN 9781427128447 (hardcover) | ISBN 9781427128522 (paperback)
Subjects: LCSH: Left and right (Psychology)--Juvenile literature.
Classification: LCC BF637.L36 F37 2021 | DDC 152.3/35--dc23
LC record available at https://lccn.loc.gov/2020049618

Crabtree Publishing Company

www.crabtreebooks.com   1-800-387-7650

e-book ISBN 978-1-947632-91-2
Print book version produced jointly with Crabtree Publishing Company NY, USA

Written by Taylor Farley
Production coordinator and Prepress technician: Amy Salter
Print coordinator: Katherine Berti

Printed in the USA/012021/CG20201102

Photo credits: Cover background © SHUTTER TOP, cover dog © Eric Isselee, cover sign © alexmillos; page 2, 3 © Jeka, page 4 © Africa Studio, page 7 © Coltty; page 8 © s_oleg; 10, 11 © Ratchanee Sawasdijira; page 13 © Alfonso de Tomas; page 14-15 © haireena; page 16-17 © ilikestudio; page 19 and 23 © Sergey Novikov; page 20-21 © Stocker_team All images from Shutterstock.com

Published in Canada
Crabtree Publishing
616 Welland Ave.
St. Catharines, ON
L2M 5V6

Published in the United States
Crabtree Publishing
347 Fifth Ave
Suite 1402-145
New York, NY 10016

Published in the United Kingdom
Crabtree Publishing
Maritime House
Basin Road North, Hove
BN41 1WR

Published in Australia
Crabtree Publishing
Unit 3 – 5
Currumbin Court
Capalaba QLD 4157